LEADER'S GUIDE

Jesus' Words for Teens

OBEDIENCE

taken from the books of
Matthew, Mark, Luke, and John
along with other relevant Bible references

Candice Mary Thomas

Published by DTJ Press
Copyright © 2018 revised 2020 Candice Mary Thomas

All images, except as noted, designed by Freepik, www.Freepik.com

No part of this book may be reproduced or transmitted in any form or by any means, electronic or mechanical, including photocopying and recording, or by any information storage or retrieval system, except as may be expressly permitted in writing by the author. Requests for permission should be emailed to dtjpress@gmail.com.

The *Jesus Words for Teens: Obedience* study is the first in the series of text courses for teens in the area of Biblical Studies.

ISBN 978-1-7332133-2-5

Scripture quotations are taken from the Holy Bible, New Living Translation, copyright © 1996, 2004, 2015 by Tyndale House Foundation. Used by permission of Tyndale House Publishers, Inc., Carol Stream, Illinois 60188. All rights reserved.

Printed in the United States of America.

Dedicated to my loving husband, Terry,
without whom I may never have accepted
Jesus Christ as my personal Lord and Savior.
Because He lives and has redeemed me,
I have a new song to sing.

Psalm 40:1-3

With many thanks and much appreciation
to Ann Hitchcock for suggestions and
Esther Yang for editing. The encouragement of
both inspired me to "keep on keeping on."

Dear Leaders,

Thank you for your willingness to serve God by mentoring our youth, leading them into a greater understanding of Scripture, God's plan for salvation, and His will for their lives. I feel it is of utmost importance for our little ones and youth to become firmly rooted in the knowledge of God's Word and in a growing love relationship with Him. When God put it into my heart to write a study based on Jesus' words, it was with the urging that these generations might see His return. Who knows? But when God calls, a believer follows. And, as the parable of the ten virgins with lamps teaches, it is always best to be prepared.

As I write from the viewpoint of one in her seventies, I readily admit that I grew up in a much more innocent age. Cigarettes and drinking might have been high school issues, but certainly not the prevalence of drugs, anxiety, depression, splintered families, gender identity issues, and the political anger and unrest we see today. Therefore, I would ask you to expand on my ideas, giving current day examples from your lives and those of others, making the questions and examples relevant to today's youth. Also, you will note that I have kept my answers brief, so please feel free to add complete details.

Guiding youth into a greater knowledge of God's Word is the path that leads to wisdom--wisdom that builds strong roots and a relationship with God, that says, "I believe You. I trust You. I will fear no evil, 'for what can man do unto me?' " **[Heb. 13:6]** So as our world grows to be more and more like that of Noah's times, we have peace because of our one great hope: the

Name of our Lord and Savior, Jesus Christ.

May each of you be blessed with a double dose of wisdom and discernment as you journey forth, teaching God's Holy Word.

Candice Mary Thomas

DEFINITIONS

General Study: Digging into God's Word, generating and writing down answers

Personal Time Discussion: Discussion of the previous week's Personal Time answers

Prayer Time: Praying for each other or country, the needs of those in other countries, ourselves, etc.

Leader's Desire: Campfire, games, visiting, more snacks, closing worship song, etc.

POSSIBLE 90-MINUTE SMALL GROUP FORMAT
4 Week Study

Opening prayer
Worship Time:	10 minutes
General Study:	20 minutes
Snack Break:	5 minutes
Personal Time Discussion:	25 minutes
Leader's Desire:	30 minutes

Eight Week Study

Alternate General Study one week with Personal Time Discussion the following week. Extend Study/Discussion Time, Snack Break, and Leader's Desire.

FAMILY STUDY

Parents: Work through the group study together. Follow up with Personal Time Discussion, being sensitive to areas that your teens may find difficult to share with you. This may prompt an opportunity for all family members to be open with each other.

(**Note:** This study uses the New Living Translation [NLT], which is easy to read and understand. Today's youth should find it relevant and relational.)

INTRODUCTION

Your preteen and teen years can be some of the most exciting years of your life. They may also bring on "growing pains"--unfamiliar emotions and questions about who you are, what lies in your future, and concern over the crazy world we live in. You may question, "How am I to live during these times?"

Being seventy, I'll admit that I grew up in a very different age. What we considered "dangerous," "risky," "stuff bad kids would do" revolved around cigarettes and alcohol. Sure, some would cheat on tests in school, stay out too late, or go on "joy rides," but all in all it was a time of innocence. You may be faced with far more troubling issues--drugs, pornography, gender identity, bullying on social media, and so much more. But you don't have to live in confusion! You have the greatest resource to give you light, direction, hope, and joy, and that is Jesus Christ. He is your answer to knowing how to live during this age.

When I was young, I wish I had known even a parcel of what I now know about Christ. What a difference it would have made! At that stage in my life, however, I only "knew" facts about Jesus. I didn't know how to live for Him, and I had no "personal relationship" with Him. It wasn't until I was thirty-two years old that I understood what this meant and asked Jesus to be my Savior. As they say, "If I'd only known...!"

This Bible study focuses on Jesus' words and what He tells us about how to live. Study His words as well as Jesus' actions. What are they, and what are they based upon? Once you know, you will understand that you have choices to make. What will they be, and how will you choose to live?

...*CHOICES*...

The *Jesus' Words for Teens...Obedience* study assumes that you have either asked Jesus to be your Savior, or you are seriously thinking of following Him. My prayer is that by the end of our journey together, you will have made many "yes" choices: "Yes, Jesus is my Savior. Yes, I want to follow Him. Yes, I believe He loves me because He made Me and will stand by me forever. Yes, I want a relationship with Him, and because I love Him, I will try my best to follow what He is teaching me. And yes, I know I will sometimes fail-- perhaps over and over--but I will always trust His amazing forgiveness and grace." **[1John 1:9]**

As you "Dig In" to God's Word, may you be blessed with inestimable joy, confidence, and trust in our awesome God, and may you grow as Jesus did, ". . . in wisdom and in stature and in favor with God and all the people." **[Luke 2:52]** And as you read your Bible, may you always remember to . . .

READ FOR WISDOM . . .
so you may
WALK IN FAITH . . .
and
LIVE TO WORSHIP!

*Throughout this study, I use the term "parent(s)" to represent whoever is raising you, whether biological or otherwise.
**All Bible verses are taken from the New Living Translation (NLT)

JESUS' WORDS
"Then Jesus said, 'Come to Me...' "
Matthew 11:28

Have you ever seen a red letter Bible where all Jesus' words are printed in red? Well, if you looked at the books of the New Testament, you'd have to think, "WOW! Jesus had a lot to say!"

Every word in the Bible has purpose. **2 Timothy 3:16** says, *"All Scripture is inspired by God and is useful to teach us what is true and to make us realize what is wrong in our lives. It corrects us when we are wrong and teaches us to do what is right."* How awesome, to have a guide for life right before our eyes!

So what did Jesus have to say, and what does He teach us? Let's "DIG IN" and take a look.

DIGGING IN--WEEK ONE--GROUP TIME

The first book in the New Testament is the book of Matthew. In it, the first words we see that Jesus said are, *"It should be done, for we must carry out all that God requires."* **[Matthew 3:15]** To find out what Jesus is talking about, read verses 13 through 15.

1. These verses are referring to Jesus' baptism.

2. Why did Jesus want this event to happen? He said this is what God required.

3. How did John react? John said that Jesus should baptize him instead.

4. Did Jesus follow John's suggestion? No, Jesus did what God asked and was baptized.

If you answered "No," then you are correct. Jesus didn't for a moment think, "Well, yeah--that's a great idea, John." He didn't give in to "peer pressure" nor was He filled with pride: "I'm God. You're not." He knew what His Father wanted. He never wavered. He did what God asked. This is what obedience looks like. It is what I call having convictions and "unshakable unbreakables," but more about that later.

For now, let's read other verses from the Bible and

discuss how they relate to Jesus' obedience.

John 4:31-34 *"Meanwhile, the disciples were urging Jesus, 'Rabbi, eat something.' But Jesus replied, 'I have a kind of food you know nothing about.' 'Did someone bring him food while we were gone?' the disciples asked each other. Then Jesus explained, 'My nourishment comes from doing the will of God, who sent Me, and from finishing His work.' "*

5. What kind of food was Jesus talking about? Talk about Jesus' life purpose--obedience to His Father--and how His death and resurrection provided salvation to all who believe.

6. Read **1 Cor. 15:22** and **1 Cor. 15: 45-49**. Summarize what work Jesus needed to finish. Talk about Adam's failure. As his "offspring," we are given physical life, but also physical death. Contrast this with Jesus, who, as the "last Adam" was the first to be raised after physical death, giving us eternal life.

Read the verses below, then explain the meaning of the phrase: *"He gave His one and only Son."*

John 3:16 *"For this is how God loved the world: He gave His one and only Son, so that everyone who believes in Him will not perish, but have eternal life. God sent His Son into the world not to judge the world, but to save the world through Him."*

Galatians 1:4 *"Jesus gave His life for our sins, just as God our Father planned, in order to rescue us from this evil world in which we live."*

7. "He gave His one and only Son" means God had a plan for Jesus' life to which Jesus was totally obedient, and that was for Jesus to give us the ultimate gift, His life, in ransom for our sins--the only way we could be reconciled with God.

8. As God had a plan for Jesus' life, does He have a plan for ours? (Read **Jeremiah 29:11** to help you answer this.) God does have a plan for each of our lives. Of course, He wants all people to be saved, for God desires that no one perish **(2 Peter 3:9)**, but He also has planned a future for each of us that is full of hope and abundant life. Have the kids talk about their talents, spiritual gifts, and deepest desires. Discuss how God uses these to give joy, to glorify Himself, and to build His kingdom on earth.

Jesus' obedience led to His death, a death more painful that we can ever imagine. Before He died, however, He did ask something of His Father. Look up **Luke 22:42a**.

9. According to this verse, what did Jesus ask His Father to do? He wanted God to take away the "cup of suffering."

10. What was the cup of suffering Jesus did not want? The torture, pain, and death He would have to endure.

In spite of this, Jesus' final statement was, "Yet I want Your will to be done, not mine." **[Luke 22:42b]** I want to bring up "unshakable unbreakables" here. Based upon convictions, "unshakable unbreakables" are commitments you make now, *before* events happen, that help you to do God's will when you face tough choices and decisions in the future.

I believe that one of Jesus' "unshakable unbreakables" was that no matter the circumstance, He would live in complete obedience to His Father. Here, for instance, Jesus knew when and how He would die, yet He was obedient to His Father and allowed each terrible moment of His capture, trials, and death to take place.

"I don't have much more time to talk to you, because the ruler of this world approaches. He has no power over me, but I will do what the Father requires of Me, so that the world may know that I love the Father. Come, let's be going." **[John 14:30-31]**

Read **Matthew 3:16-17; Mark 1:11; Mark 9:7; Luke 3:22; Luke 9:35; 2 Peter 1:17**.

11. What was God the Father's response to Jesus' obedience in all He did? "This is my dearly loved Son, who brings Me great joy. Listen to Him." Discuss this.

His Father's response must have given great strength to Jesus. It helped Him to "keep on keeping on." Always remember that *everyone* needs encouragement!

Read **Hebrews 10:1-7** below, then answer Question 11:
"The old system under the law of Moses was only a shadow, a dim preview of the good things to come, not the good things themselves. The sacrifices under that system were repeated again and again, year after year, but they were never able to provide perfect cleansing for those who came to worship. If they could have provided perfect cleansing, the sacrifices would have stopped, for the worshipers would

istock image

have been purified once for all time, and their feelings of guilt would have disappeared. But instead, those sacrifices actually reminded them of their sins year after year. For it is not possible for the blood of bulls and goats to take away sins. That is why, when Christ came into the world, He said to God, "You did not want animal sacrifices or sin offerings. But you have given me a body to offer. You were not pleased with burnt offerings or other offerings for sin. Then I said, 'Look, I have come to do your will, O God--as is written about Me in the Scriptures.' "

12. Can anyone ever offer or sacrifice enough of anything to stand in God's presence? To gain His favor and earn eternal life with Him? Why or why not? No! From the very beginning of His ministry, Jesus pointed out that He had come to earth in obedience to His Father, to give Himself as a sin offering. Because Jesus was pure, having never sinned, only He could offer this perfect "forever" sacrifice for our sins.

13. When you think on this, how important is it **to you** that Jesus followed His Father's will? Encourage teens to really think about this and answer sincerely.

Share a time of prayer with your group thanking Jesus for His obedient sacrifice. If you would like, you may write a prayer of thanksgiving or use this acrostic to praise God for His awesome plan of salvation.

T_____

H_____

A_____

N_____

K_____

Y_____

O_____

U_____

J_____

E_____

S_____

U_____

S_____

Week One--Day One--Personal Time
Think about it: Matthew 3:15 -- Jesus' Baptism

Jesus did not follow John's suggestion to baptize John. Instead, He remained totally obedient to His Father's will. Think about your life. Has there ever been a time when you were told to do something by an authority figure (parent, guardian, teacher, pastor) but were urged to do something else by your friends?

Decisions? Shouldn't I? PSSST... Let's? Should I? Choices?

Sincerely consider this question and try to think both of a time when you followed your friends' promptings and a time when you did not. Feel vulnerable? Me, too. Find it hard to admit to times when you've made wrong choices? You bet. But let's make this a "joint venture." From time to time when I ask for examples from your life, I'll give examples from both my life and from my husband Terry's. Deal? Deal.

Candice's Turn: Disobedience

I was kind of a "socially awkward" child. Braces, zits, pointy white glasses, and a tummy I couldn't quite tuck in...you get the picture! Anyway, I had a terrible time in junior high, so I begged Mom and Dad to let me go to an all-girls high school. I won this battle, and yep...that's right! No boys! (And we had so much fun!)

I wasn't really interested in dating during my freshman and sophomore years, which made my mom terribly upset. I'm not sure why, but she seemed in a hurry for me to "grow up." Finally, during my junior year, a friend set me up on a double date, and I had a great time! My date was not only cute, he was hilarious!

This guy became my boyfriend. Unfortunately, he didn't meet my mom's standards. She said he came "from the wrong side of the tracks" because he lived in a poor section of town.

Now understand that I love my mom. I will always love my mom. But she was not a Christian. She judged everything and everyone through a social, monetary lens. To her, people who counted were doctors, lawyers, dentists, etc.--people who had money and the "goods" that go along with that. But God didn't wire me that way. I pretty much liked everybody.

A high school was putting on a musical that I wanted to go to, but Mom said I couldn't. She didn't want me going anywhere with "that boy." Did I let that stop me? No way. My best friend had a plan. I would tell my mom I was going to spend the night with her, and I did. But what Mom didn't know was that my friend arranged for us to meet our boyfriends at the play. I knew this, but in not telling my parents,  I misled and deceived them. The truth was that I wanted to do what I wanted to do, regardless of my mother's direction. Sure, I wasn't about to do anything "wrong" before or after the play, but that was no excuse. So I lied. *"Remember, it is sin to know what you ought to do and then not to do it."*
[James 4:17]

Result: My mom and dad never found out about the play, so I wasn't grounded or punished in some other way. However, I did feel guilt and shame over deceiving my parents, so much so that I remember my actions to this day!

Terry's Turn: Disobedience

Eighth grade was finally ending, and I was going to celebrate by attending the graduation dance that evening at the Grange Hall in Winston, Oregon. Because we lived thirteen miles out of town, Mom gave me a ride, and I was to return home with my friend, John.

At the dance, I had such a great time square dancing, doing the polka and twist--all the modern dances of those times in 1963--that I was not ready for the night to end at 9:30! I decided to walk over to another friend's house instead of going home. **BAD CHOICE!** It was obvious that although I asked Jesus to save me a year earlier, I didn't understand placing obedience to my parents above my own desires.

At about 11:30 p.m., my friend's mom said I should head home, so I did. I walked, hitchhiked, and walked some more. As I was heading up Reston Road where I lived, there came my dad, looking for me. It was now about 1 a.m., well past curfew. Dad was boiling mad as he had been looking for me for about two hours! No one had known where I was.

Result: I got grounded and lost all my privileges for four weeks. I I was really "bummed," knowing I should have done as asked, and I ended up regretting my choice.

Your Turn: Disobedience

　　　　Give an example of a time you fell prey to peer pressure and disobeyed someone in authority over you. If you have never experienced such a time, write God a short note thanking Him for the wonderful friends He has placed in your life. These are friends who urge you to do right, even when you don't want to.

　　　　Teens write the answers on this page.

Result (if you disobeyed):

Week One--Day Two--Personal Time

Candice's Turn: Obedience

In spite of the "disobedient" example I gave you, my high school friends really were good kids. We basically stayed on the straight and narrow, but there was a time when several of them wanted me to join them in skipping a day of school to do something "fun." If I remember correctly, they were planning a trip to Lincoln City on the Oregon coast.

One of the rules in my home was that you always attended school and did your best. Grades were very important to my parents. In fact, to them, grades proved value. Not being Christians, they didn't understand that value does not come from what you do, but from who you are--a fantastic creation made in the image of God. At any rate, I bowed out of the trip with my friends so I wouldn't fall behind in my classwork.

Result of Obedience: I'll have to admit, a typical day in school with its ups and downs (you know how some classes can be . . . well . . . "yawners") but no shame or guilt over doing something I was not supposed to do.

Week One--Day Two--Personal Time

Terry's Turn: Obedience

I grew up in a non-Christian home, although we did make appearances in church at Easter and Christmas while we lived in Los Angeles, California. When I was in the fifth grade, my dad was seriously injured and forced to retire from his career as a policeman. We moved to Oregon onto eighty acres with two houses so my dad's parents could move there also.

My Grandma Zelma was a God-fearing, church-going, praying lady, and I started to go with her to a little Assembly of God church in Tenmile, Oregon. Twenty to twenty-five people attended, with two families making fifteen of the total!

Grandma led me to the Lord when I was in the seventh grade, and I was baptized in a nearby creek by Pastor Jim Black. I was so excited about Jesus, I even brought part of my Babe Ruth baseball team to church!

I loved going to church. I "led" the singing, I looked forward to praying, reading my Bible, and growing in Christ. I wanted to be a good Christian. I was taught, however, that to be a "complete" Christian, I had to speak in tongues. No matter how hard I tried, even praying at length in the private "prayer room," I couldn't! I felt I was lacking. Then something horrific happened.

During the summer of my senior year in high school, Pastor Black, who was a tree faller by trade, dropped a tree while logging. In the process, it killed his only son. Pastor never recovered from that, and within a year, he committed suicide. I thought, "If such a man of God can fall, what chance do I, 'an incomplete Christian,' have?" I was a baby Christian and didn't understand that God is a God of life--that He hates death and the evil in the world, but has to allow it due to man's free will. I didn't fully comprehend that one day, when Jesus reigns as King, justice will prevail, death will end, tears will cease, and all will be made right! So at this point, my walk in "obedience" ended, and I strayed.

For the next ten years, I didn't lead a very godly life, which got me into trouble. It wasn't until I was thirty years old that God got my attention again at a non-denominational service. Once more, in obedience to Him, I went forth at an altar call and recommitted my life to Jesus. Since that time, I've grown to understand that there is "no work" I need do to be a "complete Christian." Jesus did all "the work" with His death on the cross, and I am saved solely by my faith in Him.

Result: God completely turned my life around! He allowed me the privilege of leading Candice to Jesus. We were united, then, in bringing up our children in Him and growing in His love and Spirit. Trusting the Lord through the most difficult of times has brought us closer together, and we've now been married for almost 43 years.

Living in obedience to the Lord has been the best decision of my life. Each day as I read and study God's Word, I grow in Christ and become a better man because of the Spirit who lives within me.

Your Turn: Obedience

Teens use this area to answer.

Result of your obedience:

Teens use this area to answer.

Week One--Day Three--Personal Time

Being obedient to authority, especially without objections or excuses, is often hard in today's society. For instance, have you ever heard or said any of the following? "You can't make me! Why should I? I have rights! I should have a say in this. What I do is personal--it affects no one but me. I need to do what makes me happy."

If any of these apply to you, write what you have heard or said.

Teens answer in this area.

Why should I?   **Make me!**

I have rights!

What do you think Jesus would say to you or want you to say back to that person? God has many commands in the Bible regarding authority. Basically, we are to obey those in authority over us. When we place our will above God's commands, it's the same as deposing our Creator--King of the universe--and placing outselves above Him. We must take up our "cross" of self-denial! Every decision we make and everything we do affects others.

Week One--Day Four--Personal Time

Look up **John 12:49-50** and answer the following questions:

1. Who told (commanded) Jesus what to say? God the Father

2. Did God tell Jesus *how* to say these things? Yes

3. Why did Jesus say whatever His Father taught Him to say? God's commands lead to eternal life.

God the Father did tell Jesus exactly what He wanted Jesus to say and how He was to say it. Do you have parents who teach you to express yourself with love, respect, and kindness to others? If "yes," what kind of language do they expect you to use? What kind of topics? Tone of voice? Body language? Inclusion or exclusion of others from your conversations?

If "no," and the only language you hear is negative, swearing, bad language, etc., then remember you have a heavenly Father who loves you more that you can imagine. Turn to Him for wisdom.

"Don't use foul or abusive language. Let everything you say be good and helpful, so that your words will be an encouragement to those who hear them." **Eph. 4:29**

Your Father is teaching you that cussing and vulgar language have to go! You are never to use words that harm others, but to use words that encourage and build up others. ***Hard to do? Absolutely!*** But ask God for His help. He is faithful to answer.

"Obscene stories, foolish talk, and coarse jokes—these are not for you. Instead, let there be thankfulness to God." **Eph. 5:4**

Think and pray about God's words in **Eph. 4:29** and **Eph. 5:4** for a few minutes, then check off the following statements that apply to you:

_____ I do not use swear words.
_____ I do not use obscene language (relating to sex in an indecent, offensive way).
_____ I do not use the Lord's name in an unworthy manner.
_____ I use kind words when I talk to or about others.
_____ I include, rather than exclude, others when I speak, even if they are different from me or not in my circle of friends.
_____ My words show respect for others.

Prayerfully consider this checklist, then use it to sum up *the truth* about your habits in talking with and including or excluding others in conversation. What, if anything, do you need to change to follow **Eph. 4:29** and **5:4**?

My "Heart Check"-- *"Search me, O God, and know my heart; test me and know my anxious thoughts. Point out anything in me that offends you, and lead me along the path of everlasting life."* **[Psalm 139:23-24]**

Teens answer on this page.

Candice's Story

"#$%^&***&^%$##!!!" I heard a lot of this growing up. Cussing, swearing...add to this my brother's foul mouth... and you can imagine what kind of words swirled around in my head whenever I was annoyed. I had a choice to make--to use or not to use these words. I chose "not" and devised a plan:

* I chose non-offensive words or phrases to say when angry and practiced saying them.

* I literally said *"NO"* when offensive words came to mind and *purposely* thought of other things.

In spite of what I tried, however, nasty words occasionally blasted through my mind. True, I never said them out loud, but they were there. Then I became a Christian and learned I was not alone when wanting to change! I was a "new creation in Christ" [**2 Cor. 5:17**], and I had the Holy Spirit living within me. So I prayed for God to remove those words from my mind, and guess what? He did! It didn't happen overnight, but as time went by, I noticed I hadn't "heard" them in ages! On my own, I couldn't conquer the language of my upbringing, but with God, *"everything is possible."* [**Matt. 19:26**]

Terry's Story

While growing up in Tenmile, Oregon, I became aware of some ugly language Dad used when arguing with my mom and others who disagreed with him. I later got in trouble at school for using one of Dad's curse words and was sent to the principal's office. When Mr. McGovern asked me about it, I told him my dad used that word all the time, so it couldn't be bad, could it? He informed me that the word was indeed "bad," but because he knew my dad and how he talked, Mr. McGovern let me go back to class.

Later, during summers when I worked in the lumber mills during my late teen and college years, I was surrounded by men who used curse words. I used them, too, sometimes. It wasn't until I became a teacher that I really concentrated on not using offensive language at all. Although I wasn't walking a Christian walk, I knew that this type of language was wrong.

After marrying Candice, we remained firm in our decision not to use inappropriate language in our family. We knew the struggle it is to hear curse words and not respond in kind, and we wanted our children to use respectful language with and around others. Our children are grown now, but even today as a coach, I remind my wrestlers that cursing is not acceptable in the practice room or elsewhere.

Bad language "throws and tears down; we are to "build up."

Back to You

Want to change your language habits? Need to show more love and respect for others in your thoughts and speech? Pray right now and ask God to help you. He is your strength and the Holy Spirit your helper. And remember, your Father God will give you a full suit of armor to fight anything that is not of Him. **[Ephesians 6:10-18]**

Write your prayer here:

Teens write their prayers.

Ephesians 6:10-11 *"A final word: Be strong in the Lord and in His mighty power. Put on all of God's armor so that you will be able to stand firm against all strategies of the devil."*

DIGGING IN--WEEK TWO--GROUP TIME

As we began learning in Week One, Jesus lived a life in total obedience to His Father's will. He lived exactly as Scripture predicted so it would be fulfilled. Let's look into this some more.

Read **Matthew 5:17-20** and briefly summarize what Jesus was saying: Jesus came in obedience to fulfill *every* aspect of the law of Moses and the writings of the prophets. He was therefore going to obey *all* God's commandments, and in doing so, demonstrate true righteousness. This was in contrast to the hypocritical "righteousness" of the Pharisees.

But how did Jesus know what the commandments were--what the Father wanted of Him? Read **Luke 2:41-50.**

1. What did Jesus do? He did not leave with His parents after Passover, but stayed behind in the temple, listening and asking the teachers questions.

2. Why were the teachers amazed? They were surprised by His understanding of the Scripture and the answers He gave to their questions.

3. What does this show? Jesus had been studying Scripture and spending time in prayer with His Father God in His very early years and was now continuing to do so. He knew He needed to have knowledge and wisdom to do what His Father asked.

Read **Matthew 4:1-10** to discover a time when we are shown how Jesus put what He learned from Scripture into practice.

4. Briefly describe what happened. To take on the punishment for our sins, Jesus needed to prove Himself completely guiltless, so the Holy Spirit drove Him into the desert to be tested. There Satan tempted Jesus in areas of His humanity--turning stones into bread would meet physical needs; jumping off the pinnacle of the temple to prove His Father would protect Him would meet emotional needs; and accepting Satan's offer to immediately rule the world would fulfill the desire for power.

5. What do you learn from Jesus' responses, for example in **Matthew 4:4b**: *But Jesus told him, "No! The Scriptures say, 'People do not live by bread alone, but by every word that comes from the mouth of God.' "* Jesus countered Satan's temptations with His knowledge of Scripture. He showed how He was willing to live in obedience to His Father rather than fill short-term physical needs, emotional needs, or worldly desire. Refer to **Deut. 8:3**, **Deut. 6:16**, and the first commandment.

Let's take a moment and summarize what we've learned so far. Jesus placed His highest priority on being obedient to His Father. In order to do this, He had to fully know, understand, and value the authority of Scripture. He had to spend time in prayer with His Father. Then He could fulfill prophecy and His Father's will.

Jesus studied the Scriptures, written on scrolls, and He was continually in prayer.

The same holds true for you. Just as your body is strengthened by the food you eat, enabling you to perform physical tasks, your spirit is nourished by knowing the Word of God. It is this nourishment that gives you the strength to become obedient to your Father as He directs you. By studying, learning, and applying Scripture to your life and by spending time with God, you can grow into the kind of person He wants you to be. You will live life fulfilling the wonderful, unique destiny He has designed just for you.

Week Two--Day One--Personal Time

You probably have your very own Bible to read and learn from. Because I grew up with no Bible, I had no idea of its importance nor how it could guide my life. Once I did become a Christian, however, I couldn't spend enough time reading it. The same was true for Terry. This began an exciting time for both of us, searching for truth and personal growth.

This week I would ask you to spend time in Scripture, searching for truth regarding obedience--learning from God's Word and growing in Him. Read some of the words Jesus read. We know how they shaped His life! After reading, be sure to take time to visit with God. He is your best friend, and just like your best friend here on earth, He loves to hear what you are feeling and what you have to say. So talk to God and listen for His reply. What are you feeling deep inside...in your spirit? What would He have you know?

To begin, open your Bible to **Psalm 119** and read **verses 1-8**. For comparison, I've also printed these verses from the NLT below. Take some time in prayer, then write down what God wanted Jesus (and now you) to understand about obedience and the result it will have in your life.

"Joyful are people of integrity who follow the instructions of the LORD. Joyful are those who obey His laws and search for Him with all their hearts. They do not compromise with evil, and they walk only in His paths. You have charged us to keep Your commandments carefully. Oh, that my actions would consistently reflect Your decrees! Then I will not be ashamed when I compare my life with

Your commands. As I learn Your righteous regulations, I will thank You by living as I should! I will obey Your decrees. Please don't give up on me!" Our desire should be to consistently keep God's commands, not out of a sense of fear, but out of a sense of love for our Creator and Redeemer. When we do so, seeking God with all our hearts, and when we obey His instructions, we are given joy.

What is joy? To me, joy is internal and constant, based on complete trust in God and not on circumstances. It comes from the knowledge that God is good and always trustworthy, and it is part of the fruit of the Holy Spirit.

Is happiness the same as joy? You may wish to explore this. If happiness is viewed as the opposite of being sad, then it can be temporary and fleeting as it is being based on feelings and circumstances. However, if happiness is viewed as constant internal contentment, then it would be equivalent to joy.

Week Two--Day Two--Personal Time

Read **Psalm 119:9-16** What do these verses mean? .

We are to delight in God's decrees (commands) and not forget what He says in His Word. We are to rejoice in His laws.

Now especially consider verse 11: *"I have hidden Your Word in my heart that I might not sin against You."* Explain how we hide God's Word in our hearts.

Some ideas: 1. Keeping God's Word in our hearts and obeying it keeps us pure, clean of sin. 2. We study God's Word, sometimes reading it aloud, then thinking about it. We try to determine how we can apply it in our lives right now so we can honor God in what we say and do. 3. When we read and meditate upon God's Word, we are given delight and joy, so we desire to please Him. 4. Memorizing God's Word helps us not to sin during times of difficulty.

Week Two--Day Three--Personal Time

Have you ever gone camping, or at least been outside on a very dark night, where there are few or no lights? I have, and on occasion I have found myself in that situation without a flashlight! Stumbling around, tripping...you get the picture.

Once my husband, children, and I went camping "primitive style." That's when you have *no* toilets, *no* running water, *no* electricity, and it's pitch black at night.

I was getting ready to brush my teeth. "Water," I said, "I need some water!" I heard my saintly husband say, "This way." I headed over. "Just dip your brush in here," he said. I dipped my brush in and out, in and out, in and out...but it wasn't getting wet! What? My children and Terry burst out laughing. I had been dipping my toothbrush into the middle of a toilet paper roll!

The point is, when I have a flashlight with a strong beam, I can see where I'm going and what I'm doing. I have direction. I feel safe. I walk without stumbling--well, at least with fewer stumbles!

Read **Psalm 119:5-6**, pray, then write your thoughts on the next page about what God's Word means in your life--what it means now and what it could mean in the future.

"Your Word is a lamp to guide my feet and a light for my path."
Psalm 119:105

A beginning thought for discussion: sometimes as we grow older, we look back on former actions with regret. But if we study God's commands, know them, and are obedient to them, when we look back we will have nothing to regret. Furthermore, our actions would reflect those of Jesus and be a great witness to others.

Teens use this page to write their reflections

Week Two--Day Four--Personal Time

Read through the rest of **Psalm 119**. On what theme does every section of the Psalm center? How should you look upon God's instruction? We should delight in God's Word and respond to it with obedience. The result is delight, inner peace, and joy.

DIGGING IN--WEEK THREE--GROUP TIME
Think about it--Build on a Solid Foundation

A once strong house built on a poor foundation

Matthew 7:24-26 *Anyone who listens to my teaching and follows it is wise, like a person who builds a house on solid rock. Though the rain comes in torrents and the floodwaters rise and the winds beat against that house, it won't collapse because it is built on bedrock. But anyone who hears my teaching and doesn't obey it is foolish, like a person who builds a house on sand."*

1. What do these verses mean? They teach that we need to live with Jesus' teachings as our foundation, and having that, nothing in life can destroy us.

Read the following verses. What is Jesus teaching?

2. **Matthew 5:19b** Those who obey God's laws will be great in the Kingdom of Heaven. Be sure to discuss that this kingdom began when Jesus came to earth--that when we believe, we become part of that kingdom.

3. **Matthew 28:20** We are to teach new disciples to obey all Jesus' commands. (To do this, we must be living examples of people who live by Jesus' commands.)

4. **Luke 8:21** Jesus considers us family when we hear God's Word and obey it.

5. **John 14:15** We show our love for Jesus by obeying His commandments. Again, stress that this is not a burden, but a sign of our love for Him.

6. Okay, we are really learning a lot about the importance of obeying God's laws and commandments. But exactly which commandments does Jesus teach us to obey? To find out, write out either **Matthew 22:37-40** or **Mark 12:29-31** below.

Matthew 22:37-40 *Jesus replied, "'You must love the Lord your God with all your heart, all your soul, and all your mind.' This is the first and greatest commandment. A second is equally important: 'Love your neighbor as yourself.' The entire law and all the demands of the prophets are based on these two commandments."*

Mark 12:29-31 *Jesus replied, "The most important commandment is this: 'Listen, O Israel! The Lord our God is the one and only Lord. And you must love the Lord your God with all your heart, all your soul, all your mind, and all your strength.' The second is equally important: 'Love your neighbor as yourself.' No other commandment is greater than these."*

7. Summarize the commandment that Jesus said was the greatest and most important. Love God

8. Summarize the second commandment that Jesus said was equally important. Love people

9. On the next page, write how all the laws and demands of the prophets are summarized by these two. How can we demonstrate these? Here's a reminder of the Ten Commandments:

Exodus 20:1-17

1. *You must not have any other god but Me.*
2. *You must not make idols, bow down, or worship them.*
3. *You must not misuse the name of the Lord your God.*
4. *Remember to observe the Sabbath day by keeping it holy.*
5. *Honor your father and your mother.*
6. *You must not murder.*
7. *You must not commit adultery.*
8. *You must not steal.*
9. *You must not testify falsely against your neighbor.*
10. *You must not covet anything of your neighbor.*

Your Thoughts: The two greatest commandments are based on love. We are to first love God (commandments 1-4) and second, love people (commandments 5-10). During discussion time, talk about what it means to love God with all our hearts, souls, minds, and strength. What does that look like? Discuss loving our neighbors as ourselves and visit the topics of who we are in Christ as well as who our neighbors might be. Use the Ten Commandments as guides to your discussion.

Week Three--Day One--Personal Time

Think and pray about obedience and what that looks like in your life. Then write your thoughts on the following:

To me, obedience means . . .

Base your discussion on the teens' answers.

. . . obedience . . .

Why am I sometimes obedient and sometimes not? What would help me obey in the areas where I am struggling?

Base your discussion on the teens' answers.

Week Three--Day Two--Personal Time

Jesus said that the greatest commandment was to love God with all our hearts, souls, and minds. [**Matt. 22:38**] (Mark and Luke add "strength.") Ask yourself, "Do I really love God with all my heart? Do I really love Him with all my soul? With all my mind? With all my strength? Is there anything keeping me from loving Him with my 'all'? If so, how can I give that to God and ask for help?"

My "Heart Check":

Base your discussion on the teens' answers.

Week Three--Day Three--Personal Time

Jesus said that the second greatest commandment was like the first--to love our neighbors as ourselves. So, who is your neighbor?

Study the story of the Good Samaritan (**Luke 10:30-37**). How did the priest view the Jewish man who was beaten and robbed? The Levite? The Samaritan?

Thinking on the Samaritan's actions, ask yourself, "As a believer, how do I show others that Christ dwells in me? Who do I consider my neighbor? Do I really love others as I love myself? If I don't, why am I having a hard time loving myself and/or others? If I do, how can I show this?"

My "Heart Check": The priest and Levite may have been too calloused to help a despised Samaritan, but perhaps they didn't want to get near or touch the man because it would have made them "unclean," requiring a later, inconvenient, ritual cleansing. Review how Jesus helped lepers, the sick, the dying, and the hungry. He never considered others "beneath Him" or used inconvenience as a reason not to help. Love, mercy, and life were most important to Jesus. Visit the topic of who we are in Christ, how His Spirit helps us love and help others, and not just Christians. Be sure to address the topic of loving ourselves and how this affects our loving others. Elicit ideas on how the teens can show others love in healthy ways.

Week Three--Day Four--Personal Time

Pray and ask God to show you ways you can better love Him and/or other people. Be sure to listen to what your heart tells you. Then write down what you "hear" from your Father.

Lord, grant me wisdom as I listen and write.

My "Heart Check": Ask if God showed anyone ways to better love Him and/or others. Base your discussion on the answers.

DIGGING IN--WEEK FOUR--GROUP TIME

We have studied what Jesus asks of us regarding His commandments, but who is Jesus? Who was He and where was He before He was born in Bethlehem? Why should we follow what He teaches?

Let's take a moment to examine this, because before we can follow any of Jesus' commands, grow in Him, or live for Him, we need to know what is deep within our hearts. Our faith needs to be fully and completely ours, not that of parents, friends, or any others. So what do you truly believe about Jesus, and why? As you dwell on this, always remember that "head knowledge" is completely different from "heart acceptance" and true faith.

1. Read **Col 1:16**; **John 1:1-14, Hebrews 1:2b, and John 17:5**. What are some of the key things God wants you to know about Jesus--to understand and take deep within your heart? Jesus is God and He has always existed. Through Him, along with the Father and Holy Spirit, all things were created. Before being born into the world, Jesus was known as "the Word." He is the Word of life and He is eternal life.

Many times Jesus wants people to use their reason to determine who He is. He wants them to conclude that He is the Son of God based upon His life example and His teaching. Read, then jot down a few notes about the following passages:

2. **Matthew 22:41-45** Jesus cannot be the son of David because David himself called the Messiah "my Lord." Since the Messiah is Lord, He is the Son of God. Jesus can trace His human lineage, however, through the line of David.

3. **Matthew 9:1-7** All Israelites knew that only God could forgive sins; therefore, Jesus was telling the people that He was God.

4. **Matthew 16:1-4** Jesus was demonstrating He was God through miraculous signs, but the Pharisees and Sadducees were blinded to this. He also foretold that He would die and be resurrected in three days.

5. **Matthew 12:3-8** He (Jesus) is greater than the temple; He (Jesus) is Lord, even over the Sabbath. Therefore, Jesus is God.

6. **Matthew 11:4-6** Isaiah 45:4b-6 foretells that the Messiah, "your God . . . is coming to save you. And when He comes, He will open the eyes of the blind and unplug the ears of the deaf. The lame will leap like a deer, and those who cannot speak will sing for joy!" Jesus gives examples of performing these miracles as well as others, such as raising the dead. Thus, Jesus is telling John (and us) that He is God's Son, the promised Messiah.

7. **John 4:14** Jesus told the woman at the well that whoever drinks the water He gives will never thirst--that the water will be a well springing up to eternal life. Only God gives eternal life.

There are times, too, when Jesus either agrees with His disciples or directly tells them and the crowds that He is God. Again, read and jot a few notes about the following passages:

8. **Matthew 16:13-17** Jesus questions His disciples, asking who they think He is. When Peter states that Jesus is the Son of the living God, Jesus responds that Peter is blessed because this knowledge was revealed to him by God.

9. **Mark 14:61b-62** When the high priest, Caiaphas, asked Jesus if He was the Messiah, the Blessed One," Jesus replied that He was. He then told how He would sit at the right hand of God and would come back with the clouds of heaven. This is a direct statement from Jesus that He is God's Son.

9. **John 10:36** Jesus questions why some call it blasphemous when He calls Himself the Son of God because God set Him apart and sent Him into the world.

10. **John 11:4** Jesus states that He, the Son of God, will be glorified when He raises Lazarus from the dead.

11. **Luke 22:70** Jesus agrees with the crowd when they shout that He is stating that He is the Son of God.

After studying these verses, we see that Scripture clearly teaches through reason and statement that Jesus is the Son of God. You, then, have a most important choice to make: do you believe that Jesus is the Son of God or not? If you do believe that Jesus is God's Son, ask yourself if this is "head knowledge" or in faith, have you truly asked Jesus to be your Lord and Savior? During your personal time this week, you'll have an opportunity to pray and dwell on these questions some more.

Week Four--Day One--Personal Time

Liar, Lunatic or Lord?

C.S. Lewis popularized the saying that Jesus was either liar, lunatic, or Lord. Either Jesus was a liar, claiming He was God; a lunatic--only insane people claim they are God; or Lord, because He was God. Here are some of Lewis' words taken from his book, *Mere Christianity*: "I am trying here to prevent anyone saying the really foolish thing that people often say about Him: 'I'm ready to accept Jesus as a great moral teacher, but I don't accept his claim to be God.' That is the one thing we must not say. A man who was merely a man and said the sort of things Jesus said would not be a great moral teacher. He would either be a lunatic--on a level with the man who says he is a poached egg--or else he would be the Devil of Hell. You must make your choice. Either this man was, and is, the Son of God: or else a madman or something worse. You can shut him up for a fool, you can spit at him and kill him as a demon; or you can fall at his feet and call him Lord and God. But let us not come with any patronizing nonsense about his being a great human teacher. He has not left that open to us. He did not intend to."[1]

Spend some time today thinking about Jesus. Do you believe He was a liar? Was He a lunatic? Was and is He Lord? Explain what you believe and why.

1. Lewis, C.S. (2002) The Complete C.S. Lewis' Signature Classics. New York, NY: Harper Collins.

Your Thoughts . . . Liar, Lunatic or Lord!

Teens write their reflections on this page.

Week Four--Day Two--Personal Time

"Head Knowledge" or "Heart of Faith"

When asked if they believe in Jesus, most people will answer, "Yes." But do they just know facts about Jesus--what they've heard or been taught--or have they, by faith, accepted Jesus as Savior? Do they truly believe that Jesus is God's only Son, that He came to earth in obedience to His Father's plan; that by taking our sins upon Himself on the cross and later rising from the dead, He offered a forever blessed, eternal life to those who believe in Him?

Read the following verses about some who had "head knowledge."

Matthew 8:28-29 *"When Jesus arrived on the other side of the lake, in the region of the Gadarenes, two men who were possessed by demons met Him. They came out of the tombs and were so violent that no one could go through that area. They began screaming at Him, 'Why are you interfering with us, Son of God? Have you come here to torture us before God's appointed time?' "*

Luke 4:41 *"Many were possessed by demons; and the demons came out at His command, shouting, 'You are the Son of God!' But because they knew He was the Messiah, He rebuked them and refused to let them speak."*

James 2:19 *"You say you have faith, for you believe that there is one God. Good for you! Even the demons believe this, and they tremble in terror."*

Then there was Judas. Though he ate, traveled with, and listened to Jesus' teachings, Judas remained blinded by the love of money. True belief in Jesus never entered his heart, as witnessed by his betrayal.

Clearly, "head knowledge" alone does not change opinions or hearts. The demons recognized that Jesus was the Son of God, but they were still bent on opposing and destroying Him. And Judas turned out to be a false friend and follower of Jesus.

Now let's look at a few examples of those who developed hearts of faith when discipled or ministered to by Jesus.

The Four Gospels *The apostles*: Except for Judas, each of these men's lives were transformed during the approximately three years they traveled with, studied under, and came to believe in Jesus. Leaving lives as fishermen, tax collectors, doctors...all, filled with the Holy Spirit, rejoiced as they spread the good news of salvation in Christ. None gave up their beliefs--even when insulted, mistreated, and beaten--and all but John (and Judas, who took his own life) were brutally murdered.

Luke 8:2 *Mary Magdalene*: Once Jesus delivered Mary from the control of seven demons, she became one of His most devoted followers. Mary followed Jesus in life, and she was present with His mother and aunt at His death. Mary then witnessed Christ's empty tomb and saw Him after His resurrection.

Mark 5:2-20 *The man possessed by a legion of demons*: After Jesus removed the demons possessing this man, he longed to go with Jesus. Jesus, however, told him to return to his own people. Formerly uncontrollable, now under the influence of the Holy Spirit, this man not only returned home, but traveled throughout the decapolis (a group of ten cities), telling everyone what Jesus had done for him. Scripture says that all who heard were amazed. You can imagine the number of people who came to believe in Jesus because of this man's transformation!

Acts 9:1-31 *Paul of Tarsus*: Saul, later named Paul, was one of the greatest persecutors of Christians. After he was blinded on the road to Emmaus, hearing the voice of Jesus **(Acts 9:4)** and seeing Jesus **(Acts 9:17)**, he was completely transformed. As a missionary and writer of most of the New Testament books, Paul influenced the growth of Christianity, then and now, probably more than any other apostle. And though he suffered greatly as a witness of the Christian faith, no matter his circumstance, Paul found joy, comfort, and peace in the Lord, whom he loved and came to live for.

Now back to you. Ponder this: head knowledge tells you that Jesus is God's Son. While that is well and good, it is a heart of faith that changes you. When you have this faith, you soak in God's love--a love so great and so giving that God's only beloved Son was sent to earth to die in your place. **[John 3:16]** It is this love that flows into your life when you accept Jesus as Savior, and it is this love that transforms you.

Spend some time in prayer. Ask God to reveal to you what you really feel about Jesus--deep, deep, deep down inside. Have you truly accepted Him as your Savior? If so, have others noticed that you are a "new creature" in Him? **[2 Cor. 5:17]** If not, why not?

My "Heart Check": Teens answer here.

If you have never asked Jesus to be your Savior, or if you have done so only to please someone else, now is a great time to make the most important choice of your life. Say "yes" to Jesus and ask Him to be your Lord and Savior.

Prayer to Accept Jesus as Lord and Savior

Jesus, I have carefully considered my life, who I am without You, and who I will become with You. To change, I recognize that I desperately need You in my life, and today _____ (today's date), I, _____ (your name), am asking You to adopt me into Your family.

I know and confess that I am a sinner and recognize there is nothing I can do to rescue myself from my sins. I ask for Your forgiveness, knowing that You, pure and sinless, already willingly took those sins upon Yourself, died in my place, then rose in victory from the dead. You did all this so I can live with You forever.

So from this moment on, Jesus, I commit my life to You, asking You to rule over me as my Lord and Savior. Thank you for accepting me for who I am, but know that I am relying on Your promise to fill me with Your Holy Spirit so that I might live as a new creation, dedicated and obedient to you. Jesus, I will praise your name forever!

Already saved? Spend a few minutes in prayer, thanking Jesus for His great sacrifice and all He has done for you.

Week Four--Day Three--Personal Time

You believe in Jesus by faith, but what does that faith look like? Turn to the book of **James** and read **Ch. 2:14-25**.

1. What is James saying in these verses? He is saying that if our faith is real, alive, and well, it will be shown through the good works we do--that faith without works is dead. Have the kids ponder this idea: As Christians, God's Spirit lives within us. God is love, and love always "pours out." Therefore, when we have faith in Christ, our love "pours out" in good works.

2. Is your faith producing good works? Why or why not? Explain.

Base your discussion on the teens' answers.

3. List some of the good works you are or could be doing to show that your faith is alive.

Base your discussion on the teens' answers.

Week Four--Day Four--Personal Time

Luke 11:28 *"Jesus replied, 'But even more blessed are all who hear the word of God and put it into practice.' "*

Spend some time meditating on what you've learned and/or experienced this week, then choose one of the following:

1. Write a few words of praise to your loving and compassionate Father for His plan of salvation [**John 3:16**] and to Jesus, who fulfilled that plan by being totally obedient to His Father.

OR

2. Have you developed any convictions during your time in this study? If so, spend some time in prayer asking God if there is one or more "unshakable unbreakables" you should set based on your conviction(s). Remember that an "unshakable unbreakable" is a commitment you make now that will help you when you face tough choices and decisions, keeping in mind that Jesus, as your Savior and friend, will always be at your side to help you keep His commands.

Base your discussion on the teens' answers.

Bibliography

Bible Gateway. Version 42, Bible Gateway / Zondervan, 2016.

Holy Bible: *New Living Translation*. 2015. Carol Stream, IL: Tyndale House Publishers.

Lewis, C.S. 2002. *The Complete C.S. Lewis Signature Classics*. New York: HarperCollins Publishers.

Unger, Merrill F., and Harrison, R.K., et al., editors. 1988. *The New Unger's Bible Dictionary*. Chicago: Moody Press.

THOUGHTS / NOTES

THOUGHTS / NOTES

www.ingramcontent.com/pod-product-compliance
Lightning Source LLC
Chambersburg PA
CBHW071222070526
44584CB00019B/3121